Tip & Top

The adventures of two water drops!

Tip & Top

The adventures of two water drops!

Text and Illustrations
by Nane Annan

The American Forum for Global Education

Water!

In some parts of the world
water is just there.

You turn on the tap
and wash your hands.

You take a swim
on a hot summer day.

Rain waters flowers
and fields of wheat.

My husband Kofi Annan
cares deeply about water.
He is the Secretary-General
of the United Nations.

My husband and I taking a rest in front of a waterfall while hiking in Norway.

Water and trees are good friends.

My husband and I
are often asked to plant trees
all over the world.

We love to plant trees
but it has to be the right tree
in the right place.

Trees help clean the air.
Their roots help store water.
They also stop soil from slipping
away into rivers.

We all need water.

But in some parts of the world
there is very little.
You may have to walk
a long way to fetch water.
Maybe it comes from
a well or a hand pump,
or directly from a lake or river.

If the water is dirty,
it can harm you if you drink it.

I was sitting and thinking
of how important water is.

That was the day
I met Tip and Top.

And this is their story.

11

Tip and Top were two water drops
playing around in a river.

Top went left and Tip went right
and then they splashed together
in the middle.

The water slowed down.
The river turned into a lake.

Tip and Top started to play
a game of hide and seek.

Suddenly Tip was pulled away
into a channel.

She turned around to look for Top.
She saw him far away in the lake.

She wanted to play with him again.

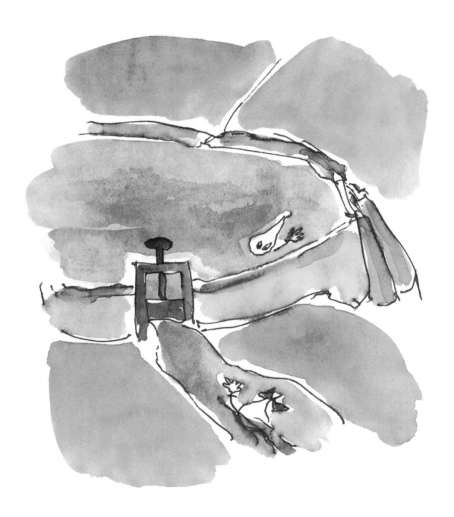

But Tip was pulled further away.

She saw large fields of rice.
Rice needs lots of water
to grow.

Water was led through
the fields in ditches
to feed the rice.

Tip tried to stay in the middle
and find her way back to the river.

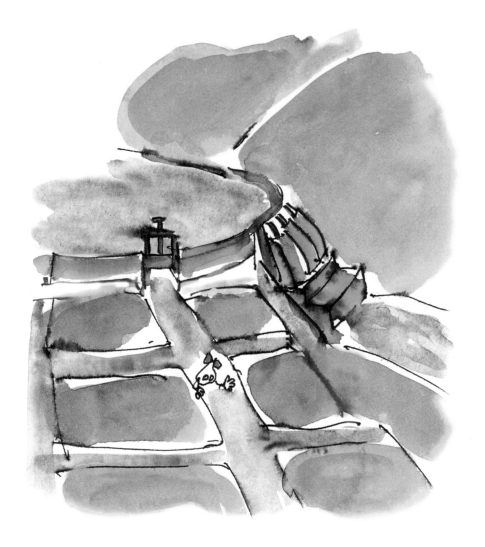

In the meantime,
Top was floating faster and faster.
He was pulled into a deep, dark tunnel.

He hit something hard.
It was a propeller.

He and all the other water drops
made it turn around.

That is the beginning of one
of the ways electricity is made!

Top was thrown out into the open.
He looked up and saw enormous tubes.

He remembered how scared <u>and</u> excited
he was coming down through them.

He saw the wires carrying
the electricity away.

He wished he could tell Tip
about everything he had seen.

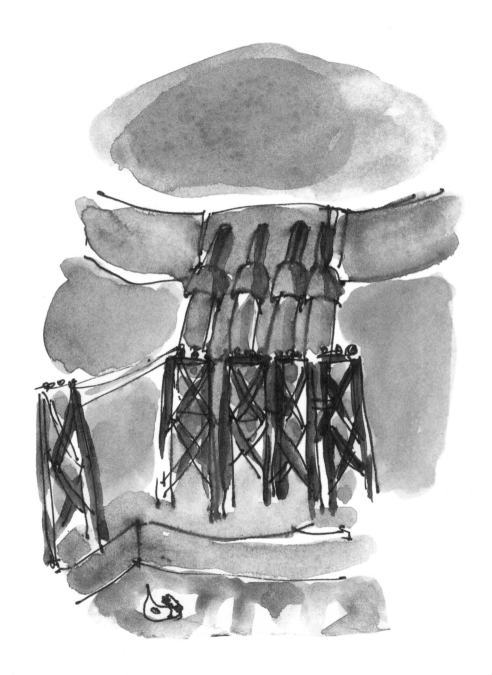

Tip was still in the rice fields.
She was almost choking
from all the chemicals in the water.

They are put there
for the rice to grow faster
and for the bugs to stay away.

But too much can make the water bad
to drink, especially for a water drop.

Tip could see the river again.

The soil was sliding down
into the river, turning it brown.

With a huge push
Tip managed to get over the edge
and back into the river.

Soon Tip had something
new to worry about.

The sun was hot and she was in
a shallow and narrow part of the river.
She was in danger of becoming mist.

At that very minute Tip saw a hole
and jumped into it.
But first she tied her red bow to a twig
just in case Top was going to come by.

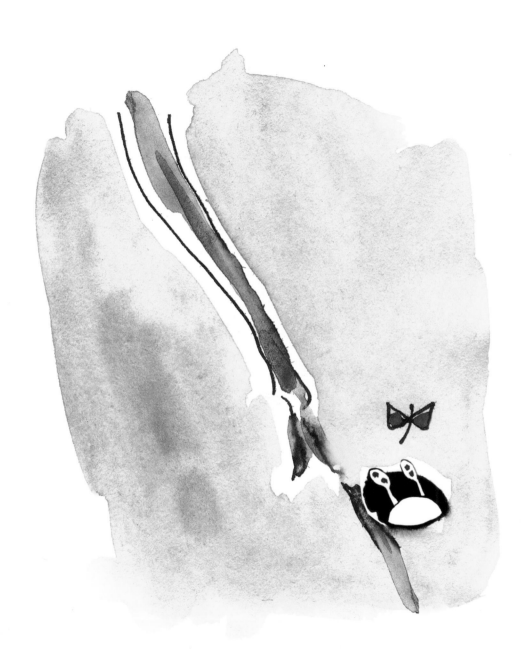

Tip did not know that she was
down in the groundwater.

It was cool and dark
and the water was clean.
She was safe,
but on the walls of the rocks
she could see the markings
from when the water was much higher.

She missed Top and the light.

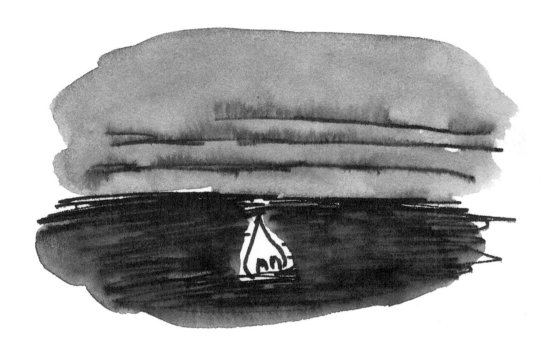

Where was Top?

He was floating down the river.

He saw how the landscape
was changing.

There were no more big trees
and the green fields were
turning brown and dry.

Then he saw Tip's red bow
tied to a twig next to a hole.

He understood immediately,
closed his eyes and jumped.
But at the last minute
he scrambled back
to bring the red ribbon
along with him.

He wished there were
NOT so many adventures!

It was very dark and he could hardly see
but he could hear somebody crying.

He whispered: "Tip"
With the echo it came back to him:
"Tip, Ti-ip"
Then he heard: "Top, To-op"

They jumped into each other's arms
and Top tied Tip's bow.

They had so much to tell each other.
They did not notice that they
were floating into a tunnel of light.

It was a well!

At that very moment a bucket
was coming down.
They rushed into it and soon
they were on their way up.

A young girl pulled up the bucket
of water and put it on her head.

She walked for miles
to bring the water home.

She had to walk back and forth
several times a day to get enough water
for her whole family.

The bucket was dirty and
Tip and Top were fighting off
germs in the water.

Germs are so small that
you cannot see them but
Tip and Top could feel them.

The girl suddenly put the bucket down
and poured some water into a cup to drink.
Tip and Top managed to jump off and
pulled some germs along with them.

They hoped that the girl would not get sick.

Tip and Top had landed
in the girl's village.

A pair of enormous shoes
walked past them.

They heard somebody say:
"The United Nations really
has to do something
so that everybody can have
safe water to drink!"

43

The weather was hot.

They were starting to feel dizzy.
The heat was turning them
into mist and they were flying up
through the air.

The next thing they knew
they hit their heads
on a cloud!

From above, the Earth looked blue.

They could see all the water.

But Tip and Top remembered
that almost all of the water
was salty and could not be used
for drinking or for plants.

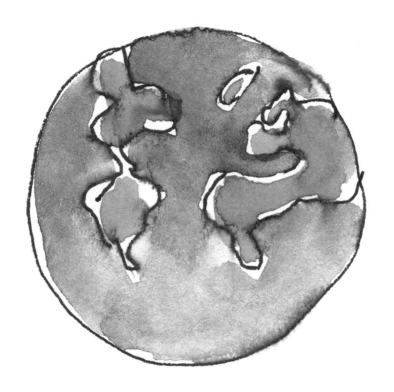

The cloud was breezing along.

It was becoming heavier and heavier
with water drops.

Just over New York and the United Nations
Tip and Top decided to let go and
fall down as raindrops.

They wanted to learn <u>everything</u>
about water.

Tip and Top tumbled down.

Three United Nations guides
stopped and smiled
and said "Hello."

Tip and Top asked politely
if anybody at the United Nations
was thinking about water.
"Oh, yes, many" said the guide from Africa.
"And right now lots of children are here
to talk about water."

The children were busy
putting their heads together
to save the water of the earth.

They wanted to give their proposals
to the leaders of the world.

The leaders of the world
had agreed in the United Nations
that many more people should
have safe drinking water.
They promised to work for
this to happen.

A boy and a girl told Tip and Top
how important it was to manage water.

Top asked: "What does that mean?"

The girl answered: "To make sure
everybody gets what they need–
even the little girl who has to walk
for miles to get water.
And you and me."
Top said: "Not me.
I <u>am</u> a water drop."

Tip and Top rushed to take the next
cloud back to the girl's village.

They wanted to tell the girl
that there was hope that

💧 she would have clean water
in a well in the village

💧 she could go to school instead
of walking so far to get water

Water is very precious.

It needs to be protected
and we should try not to waste it
so that there is enough
for all the world's people.

Everyone has to help
and to share.

What Can You Do?

Save water when you are:

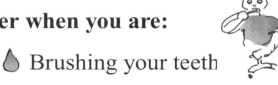

💧 Brushing your teeth

💧 Taking your bath or shower

💧 Watering your lawn

And remember!

💧 Wash your hands
especially before eating
or after using the toilet
to protect yourself from getting sick

💧 Drink plenty of clean water.
It can help you
to stay well.

Facts About Water

Can We Use All Water?

- Of all water on earth, 97.5% is salt water.
- Of the 2.5% fresh water, 70% is frozen in the polar ice caps and most of the rest is either soil moisture or deep underground.
- In fact we can use less than 1% of the world's fresh water.

Groundwater

- More than half of the fresh water we use comes from below the ground. We call this groundwater. We are using so much of the groundwater that its level is going down in many places.
- If sewage treatment plants are not working well or do not exist, the groundwater can become dirty and dangerous for human use.

Finding Water

- One out of every six people in the world—altogether 1 billion people—has no clean water to drink. 2.4 billion people, almost half of the world's population, have no toilet to use.

- If you drink unsafe water or cannot wash your hands before eating, you can get sick.

- When families do not have water at home, women and girls usually have to fetch and carry water – often over long distances. How much water do you use every day? How much would you be able to carry home if the closest well was half an hour away?

- Leaders of the world have agreed to reduce by half the proportion of people without access to safe drinking water by the year 2015. You can follow the progress on the United Nations Website: www.un.org

World Water Day

- World Water Day is celebrated every year on March 22. Each year, the United Nations decides on a different theme. You can go to www.worldwaterday.org for more about that day.

WaterYear2003

Tip and Top support the International Year of Freshwater 2003.
For more information on the year log on to www.wateryear2003.org

Acknowledgements

First of all, I want to thank David Finn for his unwavering enthusiasm in making sure that my ideas come to fruition; Susan Slack for her kindness in general and for her help in editing in particular; Gail Garcia for tirelessly and creatively working with me on the design; my appreciation to my friends of water for their support and advice when reading the script as it was coming along. And finally a warm thank you to Andy Smith and the American Forum for Global Education for again taking on a project that they believe in with the aim of reaching as many children as possible.

Profits from the sale of this book will be donated to UNICEF.

Copies are available from:
The American Forum for Global Education
120 Wall Street, Suite 2600
New York, NY 10005
(212) 937-9092

Illustrations by Nane Annan.
Photo Credits: Page 5: Photograph by Øystein Dahle. Page 7: *top and middle:* UN Photos by Eskinder Debebe;
bottom: UN Photo by Sergey Bermeniev; Page 9: *top*: UNICEF/HQ92-1294/ Roger Lemoyne; *middle:* UNICEF/C59-15 Maggie Murray-Lee
bottom: UNICEF/HQ95-0066/Jonathan Shadid; Page 11: Photo by Kofi Annan; Back Cover: UNICEF/HQ97-1187/Giacomo Pirozzi.